D1064218

Wild Flowers of America

BY
JANE HARVEY

Illustrations by
IRVING LAWSON

WHITMAN PUBLISHING COMPANY
RACINE, WISCONSIN

W 737

INTRODUCTION

It is the purpose of this little volume to describe briefly and in simple, untechnical language, the outstanding characteristics of some of the most common of the wild flowers of our United States. In doing this, we fully realize our limitations; but we hope that the descriptions and their accompanying pictures may enable the interested observer to identify the plants which he sees in his walks and stimulate his further interest in wild flowers.

We hope, also, that this interest, further stimulated, may lead him to such books as Asa Gray's Botany, available in any good library, to F. Schuyler Mathews' "Fieldbook of American Wild Flowers," and to other books of detailed and technical descriptions.

A walk through the woods and fields, over the mountainsides or hillsides, is vitally interesting to anyone who is equipped with enough knowledge of the different plants to identify those which he happens upon. It is like meeting old friends. Then, too, there is the added zest of finding new plants to identify.

People who study wild flowers grow to love and appreciate them; they are never ruthless or destructive in their zeal for collecting. Some of our most beautiful specimens have been almost wiped out by the greedy barbarians who strip whole localities before they are satisfied.

It is well to remember that, while the wild flower is beautiful in its habitat, it affords only a very transient pleasure when transferred to a vase or basket.

Jane Harvey

March, 1932.

Copyright 1932
Whitman Publishing Co., Racine, Wis.
Printed in U.S.A.

CAT-TAIL FAMILY
(Typhaceae)

A marsh family with perennial roots. Very graceful and much admired by artists. Flowers have no corolla or calyx.

NARROW-LEAVED CAT-TAIL (*Typha angustifolia*), has a narrow leaf and its two groups of flowers are separated on the flower-spike by a short distance. It is not so large in diameter as the broad-leaved cat-tail. Found in extreme Northeast, south, and as far west as Michigan and Missouri. Blossoms June-July.

CAT-TAIL (*Typha latifolia*), is common in marshes everywhere. The leaves are flat, sword-shaped, light green and usually grow higher than the flower-stem. The upper part of the long, cylindrical flower-spike bears the stamens and is of a yellowish-brown color; the lower part bears the pistils and is the familiar brown cat-tail. Fruit is dry and nut-like. Blossoms June-July.

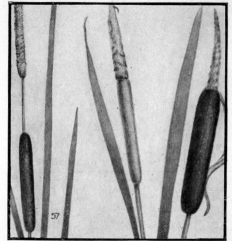

NARROW-LEAVED CAT-TAIL

CAT-TAIL

3

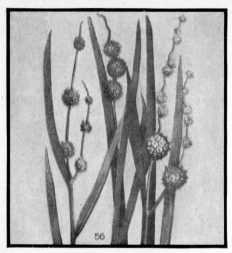

GREAT BUR REED

BUR REED FAMILY
(Sparganiaceae)

Found in damp places like marshes or along the edges of inland waters. Flowers are arranged in spherical clusters. Insects and flies common to marshes, assist in its fertilization.

GREAT BUR REED *(Sparganium eurycarpum)*, like the cat-tail, bears two kinds of flowers which are contained in separate groups along the stems. It is a tall, upright plant with its flowers arranged in heads along the upper part of the leafy stem. Later, the heads become bur-like spheres. The leaves are long and narrow, shaped like ribbon bands and of a deep green color. They, too, are quite similar to those of the cat-tail. The plant grows from three to seven feet high and is found along the edges of rivers and stagnant pools everywhere in the United States. Blossoms June-August.

WATER PLANTAIN FAMILY
(Alismaceae)

The Water Plantain Family is noticeable for its leaves which are artistic in form and of a lovely shade of green. The pure white or pink flowers have yellow centers and are also very beautiful.

NARROW-LEAVED ARROWHEAD (*Sagittaria Engelmanniana*), has very narrow leaves. Grows in shallow water. The flowers are very small. Blossoms August-September.

ARROWHEAD (*Sagittaria latifolia*), found in sluggish waters and quiet streams. The leaves of this beautiful water plant are deep, shining green, shaped like an arrowhead, growing on long stems from the plant root. The flowers are pure white, three-petaled, with deep, golden centers, arranged in whorls of three on an upright flower-stalk. Blossoms July-September.

NARROW-LEAVED ARROWHEAD   **ARROWHEAD**

5

SKUNK CABBAGE

ARUM FAMILY
(Araceae)

The members of this family have a peppery juice. Indians are said to have boiled the roots of the Jack-in-the-pulpit and eaten them. Hence the nickname "Indian Turnip."

SKUNK CABBAGE (*Symplocarpus foetidus*), is found in the extreme Northeast, south to North Carolina and westward to Minnesota and Iowa, in bogs and swamps. It is interesting because of its unusual appearance and disagreeable odor, which is attractive to certain insects. It has a thick spadix* with pinkish-lavender flowers, set inside a green and purple hood. The ovate, heart-shaped leaves are short-stemmed and appear after the flowers have started to fade. Blossoms March-April.

* Spadix—a spike with a fleshy axis.

ARUM FAMILY (Cont.)
(Araceae)

JACK-IN-THE-PULPIT *(Arisaema triphyllum)*, is the most common and best loved of the Arum Family. It grows in dense, moist woods and along woodland borders, taking on a purple shade in its natural abode and growing paler when exposed to the bright sunlight. It derives its name from the fact that its spathe resembles the pulpits of an early period, which had "hoods" over them. The spadix, or spike, stands erect under a hood of pale green, striped with purplish-brown and has clusters of flowers near its base—naked above. Its leaves grow on long stems and are of a dull green color striped with brown. Each leaf is divided into three parts and rises above the flowers that are sheltered by the hood. Blossoms April-June. Later, it bears clusters of brilliant red berries. The most beautiful specimens are found in the depths of moist and thick woods.

JACK-IN-THE-PULPIT

DAY FLOWER   **SPIDERWORT**

SPIDERWORT FAMILY
(Commelinaceae)

Herbs with sticky juices and leafy stems.

DAY-FLOWER (*Commelina communis*), is a door yard species, sometimes called "Asiatic Day Flower"; it has light blue flowers, a heart-shaped spathe and leaves which are lance-shaped. The flower has three rounded petals, the two lateral ones larger than the odd one, enclosed in the spathe. Blossoms open for a day, only. Found, Delaware to Florida, west to Kansas and Texas on moist banks. Blossoms from June-October.

SPIDERWORT (*Tradescantia Virginiana*), is found in rich ground from Maryland southward and as far west as the Rockies. Has erect stems with pale green, long and narrow leaves. Flowers have three blue petals. Blossoms May-August.

LILY FAMILY
(Liliaceae)

The Lily Family is a large one, whose members differ greatly in appearance. The asparagus and wild leek are two of the ordinary members. They are mostly perennial herbs quite noticeable for the loveliness of their flowers.

LARGE FLOWERING TRILLIUM *(Trillium grandiflorum)*, bears, at the summit of its stem, a solitary, beautiful, white flower with three petals curving backward and turning pink as the flower ages. Its leaves are ovate, broad, dark green, sharp at the point and narrowed at the base. They grow in a whorl below the flower. It thrives in moist, rich soil from New England States, west to Minnesota and south to North Carolina. Blossoms May-June. Develops reds berries.

LARGE FLOWERING TRILLIUM

LILY FAMILY (Cont.)
(Liliaceae)

YELLOW MEADOW LILY

YELLOW MEADOW LILY *(Lilium Canadense)*, is found in low meadows from extreme Northeast, south to Georgia, west to Minnesota, Nebraska, and Missouri. Has lance-shaped leaves growing in circles about the stalk. The flower, which is pendulous, is bell-shaped, deep yellow or orange on the inside, freckled with brown spots, lighter yellow on the outside. Usually there are several of these beautiful flowers, each on a long stem, at the summit of the plant. Wild bees sip the honey from the flower cup of this lily which retains its nectar until the bee draws it out. This is possible because the hanging position of the flower prevents the rains from diluting or washing away the nectar. Sometimes the bee, in its efforts, will agitate the lily-cup until it swings, as though it were in a breeze. Blossoms June-July.

85

LILY FAMILY (Cont.)
(Liliaceae)

FALSE SOLOMON'S SEAL *(Smilacina stellata)*, is sometimes confused with "Spikenard." Flowers are white and few in number, clustered about the end of the stem. Leaves are fastened close to the stalk and grow one above the other, on either side of it. Found in moist places and meadow lands, extreme northeast to Minnesota and south. Blossoms May-June.

DOGTOOTH VIOLET; YELLOW ADDER'S TONGUE *(Erythronium Americanum)*, is found in moist woods, in extreme Northeast, south to Florida and as far west as Arkansas. It bears a solitary, yellow flower which is lily-like and divided into six parts. Its leaves are two in number, greyish-green and mottled with darker color or closely dotted. They grow from the base of the plant. Blossoms April-May.

FALSE SOLOMON'S   DOGTOOTH VIOLET
SEAL

11

BLUE FLAG

IRIS FAMILY
(Iridaceae)

The Iris is an herb found in damp places. Has bulbous roots. Flowers are beautiful in shape and color.

BLUE FLAG; FLEUR-DE-LIS *(Iris versicolor)*, bears a solitary flower which rises from a green spathe at the end of the flower stalk. It has broad, violet sepals, veined with purple over white with yellow showing at the base. Petals are erect. Leaves are straight, sword-shaped and flat, of a bluish green color. The plant, its leaves and its flowers are all very decorative and much used by artists because of the grace and beauty of form and color. It is found in swamps and on wet banks from the extreme Northeast, south and west to Arkansas and Nebraska. Blossoms May-July.

IRIS FAMILY (Cont.)
(Iridaceae)

BLUE-EYED GRASS *(Sisyrinchium angustifolium)*, grows among the meadow grasses. Its flower is of an intense blue and has a center which is white and star-shaped; has six divisions and each one is armed with a thorn-like point. Its leaves are long, narrow and pale green in color. Found extreme Northeast, south to Virginia and westward. Blossoms May-July.

NARROW BLUE FLAG *(Iris prismatica)*. This species of iris has very narrow leaves, blue flowers and a long, slight stem. It is found in wet places from Maine to Pennsylvania as far south as Georgia. Flowers are smaller — having narrower measurements. Fruit is a slender capsule, sharply angled. Blossoms May-June.

BLUE-EYED GRASS   NARROW BLUE FLAG

YELLOW LADY'S SLIPPPER

ORCHID FAMILY
(Orchidaceae)

This family is very large and very difficult to analyze. The flowers are striking in color and unusual in form. Some of the most beautiful species are becoming rare in states where they used to be fairly common.

YELLOW LADY'S SLIPPER; MOCCASIN FLOWER *(Cypripedium parviflorum)*, is one of the most striking members of the Orchid Family. It is tall, with a slender, leafy stem. The lip of the flower is shaped somewhat like a moccasin or wooden shoe and is of a brilliant golden-yellow, spotted with purple. The petals are narrow, twisted and of a greenish color, streaked with purple. Found in woods and shady bogs from extreme Northeast, south to Alabama and westward. Blossoms May-July.

14

ORCHID FAMILY (Cont.)
(Orchidaceae)

SHOWY LADY'S SLIPPER (*Cypripedium hirsutum*), is considered the loveliest of the whole Orchid Family. It has a stout, leafy stem, also hairy. Flower has lip, much inflated, white in background, overlaid with soft, red markings. Its petals and sepals are white and broad. Its leaves are ovate, terminating with sharp angles. Because of its rare beauty, this species has been much sought and as a result of its popularity, is very scarce in many localities where it was once abundant. It has been successfully transplanted into domestic gardens, by expert methods. Blossoms June-July. It thrives in damp woods and swamp lands from extreme Northeast, southward to Georgia and westward to Minnesota.

The species C. reginae was named as Minnesota's state flower.

SHOWY LADY'S SLIPPER

15

ORCHID FAMILY (Cont.)
(Orchidaceae)

INDIAN PINK   **GRASS PINK**

ARETHUSA-INDIAN PINK (*Arethusia bulbosa*), has a solitary blossom of magenta-pink, terminating its slender stem. The lip of the flower turns down and is ribbed with three white crests; edge is wavy and spotted, sometimes with deep pink or red. Found in swamps and boggy lands from extreme Northeast, south to South Carolina, westward to Minnesota. Blossoms May-June.

GRASS PINK (*Calopogon pulchellus*), is a slight-stemmed, dainty member of the Orchid Family, bearing pink flowers at the top of its stalk. The flower has a lip covered with different colored hairs. One green, long and narrow leaf rises from the base, after the blossoming season has passed. Thrives in swamps and boggy lands from extreme Northeast to the Gulf and west to Minnesota. Blossoms June-July.

ORCHID FAMILY (Cont.)
(Orchidaceae)

NODDING POGONIA (*Pogonia Triantho-phora*), has a delicate flower of magenta shade that nods from the angle formed by the leaf joining the slender stem. The flower has a lip of three lobes and is solitary. The small, green leaves alternate and are stemless. Thrives in Vermont, south to the Gulf and west to Wisconsin. Blossoms August-September.

SHOWY ORCHIS (*Orchis spectabilis*), is what its name implies. Two shining, green leaves rise from the base of the stalk and form a sheath for the magenta-pink flowers. Petals and sepals are arranged to form a hood; beneath the hood is a whitish lip which turns downward and has a spur back of it. Within this spur, nectar is stored to tempt the bees and other insects. This species is found in rich, deep woods from Maine south to Georgia and west to Missouri and Dakota. Blossoms May-June.

NODDING POGONIA   SHOWY ORCHIS

17

BIRTHWORT FAMILY
(Aristolochiaceae)

PIPE VINE (*Aristolochia macrophylla*) commonly called "Dutchman's Pipe," is a climbing vine with kidney-shaped leaves, almost smooth, broad and deep green. Flowers are greenish-yellow with a brownish-purple, flat border; curved tube resembles a pipe. Found in Pennsylvania, south, and west to Minnesota. Blossoms May to June.

WILD GINGER (*Asarum Canadense*) has a soft, kidney-shaped leaf, somewhat pointed at the end, with woolly surface carried on long stem from base of plant. Bears a solitary flower, bell-shaped calyx whose lobes spread at the top and are of a purplish-brown color. Found in rich soils of woods. extreme Northeast southward to Carolina, common in North west, Missouri and Kansas. Blossoms April and May.

PIPE VINE   **WILD GINGER**

18

PINK FAMILY
(Caryophyllaceae)

EVENING LYCHNIS (*Lychnis alba*), is a species of the Pink Family which grows in gardens and waste places, opening in the evening. The flower is white or pinkish, deeply indented on the edge of each petal. It has inflated calyx, with pink ridges. Slight fragrance. Has dark green leaves, lance-shaped and hairy, growing opposite each other along the stalk. Extreme Northeast to New Jersey and westward. Blossoms July-September.

BOUNCING BET (*Saponaria officinalis*), called "soap-wort"; bears rose-pink flowers, clustering at the stem ends. Its leaves are ovate, perpendicularly ribbed. Very lovely. Found in waste places and also in door yards. Spicy-fragrant. Juice is sticky and "suds" in water; hence the name "soapwort"; also Latin name from "sapo" meaning soap. Blossoms July-September.

EVENING LYCHNIS   BOUNCING BET

19

SPRING BEAUTY

PURSLANE FAMILY
(Portulacaceae)

The members of the Purslane Family are low-growing, with thick leaves, found in damp woods. The flowers are not symmetrical, having fewer sepals than petals.

SPRING BEAUTY *(Claytonia Virginica)*, is named for John Clayton, an early botanist who lived in Virginia. It has a small, dainty flower of pale rose-pink, veined with a deeper pink. Flower has five petals and only two sepals. The leaves are deep green, long and slender, clasping the stalk about midway. It blossoms among the very first of the wild, spring flowers. The Spring Beauty, because of its nectar, is a great favorite of the bumble bee and other thirsty insects. It thrives in moist sunny woods in extreme Northeast, westward to Wisconsin, and south to the Gulf. Blossoms March-May.

WATER LILY FAMILY
(Nymphaeaceae)

The Water Lily Family is small, but outstanding because of its beautiful flowers. Its members are aquatic herbs, perennial, the leaves of the plant floating on the water. The solitary flower is wax-like and lovely.

WATER-LILY *(Castalia odorata)*, is found in quiet waters everywhere. It has a very large, white, sweet-scented flower of wax-like appearance, which opens in the morning and closes later in the day. Flowers have many petals, arranged in rows, with stamens of bright gold color. Leaves are circular, heart-shaped at base, deeply cleft, smooth margin without toothing, dark green on upper surface and pinkish below. In some localities, this species of water lily is raised in artificial ponds for commercial purposes. It is also a favorite subject with artists. Blossoms June-September.

WATER LILY

WATER LILY FAMILY (Cont.)
(Nymphaeaceae)

YELLOW POND LILY (*Nymphaea advena*), grows above the water or floats, and has erect leaves which are thick and roundish. Its flowers are yellow with six sepals which are yellow inside, green outside, arranged so as to overlap each other and form a cup-shaped hollow in which the stigma shows, a golden-yellow disk. Blossoms May-September in quiet waters. Odorless. Found Vermont, southward and westward to Wisconsin.

SMALL YELLOW POND LILY (*Nymphaea microphylla*), is a very slender species with round, kidney shaped leaves, thin and submerged; and broad, elliptical leaves floating. Flowers are very small, golden yellow with dark red disc. This small lily is found in still and slow-moving streams from Maine to Pennsylvania and northwest. Blossoms June-September.

YELLOW POND LILY

CROWFOOT FAMILY
(Ranunculaceae)

RUE ANEMONE (*Anemonella thalictroides*), a delicate, early spring flower to be found in partially shaded places. The blossom rises on its stem from a whorl of leaves and is pinkish outside, whitish inside. Has four to nine delicate sepals and blooms in clusters of from two to three flowers. Everywhere. Blossoms March-May.

WOOD ANEMONE; WIND FLOWER (*Anemone quinquefolia*), has a solitary flower, deep pink or magenta-tinged—sometimes white—delicate, most frequently with five petals. Three deep green leaves, divided into five parts, grow about a third of the way down the stem. Blossoms April-June—along the edges of wooded lands from extreme Northeast, south to Georgia, and west to Rockies.

RUE ANEMONE　　WOOD ANEMONE

CROWFOOT FAMILY (Cont.)
(Ranunculaceae)

MARSH MARIGOLD (*Caltha palustris*), has heart-shaped, dark green leaves and lovely, gold colored flowers. Flowers usually have five sepals (sometimes more) and many very bright stamens. Stems are hollow. Found, as name implies, in marshes and wet grounds. Blossoms April-June. Extreme Northeast, south to South Carolina and west to Nebraska. Often mistakenly called "cowslip."

SWAMP BUTTERCUP (*Ranunculus septentrionalis*), grows in moist, damp places everywhere. It has a hollow stem and its dark green leaves are divided into three leaflets. Where the flower-stems branch from the stalk, there are three leaves which are green, long and narrow with smooth edges. The flower is yellow—one on a stem. Blossoms April-July.

MARSH MARIGOLD   SWAMP BUTTERCUP

CROWFOOT FAMILY (Cont.)
(Ranunculaceae)

HEPATICA; LIVERWORT *(Hepatica triloba)*, comes very early in the spring, flowering before the leaves appear, in the open, woodland spaces. The flower has light purple sepals; its stems are hairy and its leaves are dark green, having three lobes. These leaves last through the winter, new and lighter ones appearing in the spring. Extreme Northeast, west to Minnesota and Missouri, south to Florida. Blossoms March-May.

COLUMBINE *(Aquilegia Canadensis)*, is found on rocky slopes and on the shady edges of woods. The light green leaves have three divisions or leaflets. It is a slender, branching plant and bears pendulous, scarlet flowers, yellow inside, the petals forming five tubes ending in red spurs which contain nectar. Stamens are yellow and long. Blossoms April-July.

HEPATICA   COLUMBINE

89

MANDRAKE

BARBERRY FAMILY
(Berberidaceae)

The Barberry Family has both herbs and shrubs. A member of this family, "Oregon Hollygrape," was named state flower for Oregon. The fruit of this family comes in the form of a berry or a pod with few seeds.

MANDRAKE *(Podophyllum peltatum)*, commonly called "May-apple," has a beautiful, wax-white flower of six petals which grows lower on the stalk than the green leaves. The flower-stem, bearing the solitary flower, emerges from the fork formed by the joining of the leaf-stems to the plant-stalk. Flower has sickish odor and the lemon-shaped fruit which follows, has sickish flavor. Leaves and roots are poison. Grows in moist, rich wood from New York, west to Nebraska and southward. Blossoms April-May.

POPPY FAMILY
(Papaveraceae)

The members of the Poppy Family are bristly-hairy herbs, most of them bearing beautiful flowers of vivid red, yellow or white. The sap is extracted from some of the plants and used in drugs for medicinal purposes.

BLOODROOT *(Sanguinaria Canadensis),* is found early in the spring in rich woodlands or along their edges. Its flower usually has eight, pure white petals, with a bright golden center. The stem "bleeds" when broken and the root, also, has a reddish juice. When the plant first comes up, the leaf is wrapped about the flower-bud. The flower pushes its way up beyond the leaf and terminates a slender stem. Root is used for medicinal purposes. Blossom is very transient, blowing away soon after opening. Common. Blossoms April-May.

BLOODROOT

POPPY FAMILY (Cont.)
(Papaveraceae)

CALIFORNIA POPPY

CALIFORNIA POPPY (*Escholtzia Californica*), is worthy of mention as one of the most beautiful of our wild flowers. It is typical of California sunshine and so beloved by the people of California that they have named it their state flower. It thrives on mountain sides and in valleys. Other states cultivate it for gardens where it blooms profusely and seeds itself year after year. It has four bright yellow petals, sometimes with a tinge of red at the base. Its leaves are lace-like and pale green.

CELANDINE POPPY (*Stylophorum diphyllum*), has pale green leaves divided into lobes and deep yellow flowers of four petals sometimes arranged in clusters, usually solitary. Blossoms May in damp woods. West Pennsylvania to Wisconsin, Missouri and Tennessee.

FUMITORY FAMILY

(Fumariaceae)

The members of this family have a peculiarly shaped flower. Among the most beautiful of them is the one commonly called:

DUTCHMAN'S BREECHES *(Dicentra cucullaria)*, named because of its remote resemblance to a pair of dutchman's breeches. Its flowers grow upon very short stems, strung along a stalk that rises above the leaves of the plant. They hang pendant and nod in the wind. Their petals are four in number, pure white and arranged in pairs; the larger pair is joined together and forms a heart-shaped sac, while the smaller pair is arranged about the stamens. The leaves are silver-green, finely cut and divided into three leaflets. Habitat, in the shade, sometimes on the edges of woods—southern part of New York, south to North Carolina, west to Missouri and Minnesota. Blossoms April-May.

DUTCHMAN'S BREECHES

COMMON or BLACK MUSTARD

MUSTARD FAMILY
(Cruciferae)

Is a very large and natural family of non-poisonous plants.

The members of this family are herbs with strong and pungent juices. It takes its Latin name from the word "crux" meaning cross, because of the cross arrangement of the four opposite petals of the flowers. The flowers are very ordinary in their color and size.

COMMON OR BLACK MUSTARD *(Brassica nigra)*, is a farm pest, very difficult to eradicate. It is hairy and bears small, pale yellow flowers, which grow in clusters that terminate the stems. Seed is valuable as a commercial product in manufacturing condiments and remedies. Leaves are variously lobed, saw-edged, the terminal lobe being largest. Found everywhere in fields and pastures and along highways. Blossoms June-September.

PITCHER PLANT FAMILY
(Sarraceniaceae)

The plants of this family grow in peat bogs and swamps and bear leaves of very unusual shape.

PITCHER PLANT; INDIAN DIPPER; SIDE-SADDLE FLOWER; HUNTSMAN CUP (*Sarracenia purpurea*). The dull pink petals of this flower fold together, protecting the pollen. The five sepals are madder-purple in color, of a greenish shade inside. The leaves are pitcher-shaped and hold water in which insects frequently drown; they grow about the base of the plant in a circle, are hollow and covered inside with fine hair which droops downward and makes it hard for the insect, once inside, to escape. The bodies of these insects are said to nourish the plant. Blossoms May-June from extreme Northeast, south to Florida, Kentucky and through the Great Lakes Region.

PITCHER PLANT

ORPINE FAMILY
(Crassulaceae)

The members of the Orpine Family consist of succulent herbs which bear perfectly symmetrical flowers, small in size. Leaves are mostly sessile.*

LIVE-FOREVER; GARDEN ORPINE *(Sedum purpureum)*, has purple flowers which cluster at the top of the strong, pale, erect, green stems. The leaves are thick and fleshy and of a silver-green color. Widely cultivated in rock gardens and as borders for flower beds. Common. Blossoms June-September. (The word "sedum" is taken from the Latin word meaning "to sit" and is applied to these flowers because of their tendency to fix themselves on rocks.) This species is an escape from civilization. It is a perennial and flourishes with very little care, blooming throughout the summer months. Children like to make "purses" out of the fleshy leaves.

*Without footstalk.

LIVE-FOREVER

ROSE FAMILY
(Rosaceae)

This is a very interesting family because of the beauty of its flowers. Most of them are fragrant and yield a honey of finest flavor. The raspberry, strawberry, cloudberry, the pear and the apple etc., all belong to this family, most of whose members are trees and shrubs, although there are a great many herbs, also.

SWAMP ROSE *(Rosa Carolina)*, is a very beautiful specimen. It is bushy and its leaflets are olive-green with notched edges—sharp at each end and usually hairy underneath. They are very ornamental. Its deep pink flowers grow in clusters and are followed by a red fruit, somewhat resembling a tiny apple. Grows in low ground on the borders of swamps and streams; thorny. Blossoms June-July. Common.

SWAMP ROSE

ROSE FAMILY (Cont.)
(Rosaceae)

SWEETBRIER ROSE *(Rosa rubiginosa)* has a sweet-scented leaf. The fragrance is penetrating and resembles an apple scent. Its flowers are pink and grow in clusters. Found in dry, barren pastures and waste places everywhere. Its stems reach out and arch over very gracefully. It is equipped with prickles. Its leaflets are sharply toothed and resinous underneath. Ornamental; cultivated in yards. Blossoms June-July.

PASTURE ROSE *(Rosa humilis)*, is low growing, usually showing solitary flowers, five petals, pink with golden centers—at the ends of the stems. Its leaflets are dark green, usually duller and thinner than some of the species. Is thorny and grows in dry, rocky places. Blossoms June-July. Nova Scotia to Florida, west to Minnesota and southward.

SWEETBRIER ROSE   PASTURE ROSE

PULSE FAMILY
(Leguminosae)

Clovers, peas, and beans are among the common members of this family.

BLUE LUPINE (*Lupinus perennis*), is one of the loveliest of wild flowers. The blossom is shaped like a pea blossom, shading from violet to purple. It is very showy; grows in sandy fields everywhere. Blossoms May-June.

COMMON VETCH (*Vicia sativa*), climbs something like the pea-vine of our gardens. In Canada and parts abroad, vetch is cultivated as animal fodder. Its flowers are purple and grow in pairs or singly at the place where the plant-stem and leaf-stem meet. Its leaflets are arranged on either side of the stem which has two tendrils at the end. These catch hold and twine about objects near at hand. Common in dry places. Blossoms May-August.

BLUE LUPINE

GERANIUM FAMILY
(Geraniaceae)

HERB ROBERT   **WILD GERANIUM**

HERB ROBERT *(Geranium Robertianum)*. Ornamental species with reddish-purple flowers, decorative leaves and a strong odor. Grows in moist woods and shady places from Minnesota, New Jersey, Pennsylvania, and Missouri. Blossoms June-October.

WILD GERANIUM or CRANESBILL *(Geranium maculatum)*, is a frail, lovely wild flower, colored a very light purple with a pinkish tinge. The flowers grow in clusters of a few, at the ends of the stems. They have large petals, arranged so that they overlap slightly. The leaf has five lobes, is hairy and very coarse with a fuzz on its surface; also mottled. It grows in woods and beside roads from Northeast to South and West. Blossoms May-September.

SORREL FAMILY
(Oxalidaceae)

Low-growing herbs with a sour juice and regular, perfect flowers.

WHITE WOOD SORREL (*Oxalis Acetosella*), is very pretty and of a delicate appearance. Grows in cool, damp places; its leaves, composed of three leaflets, close every evening. Dainty flowers are pinkish-white, deeper pink-striped. Blossoms May-July—in the extreme Northeast and in mountains of North Carolina.

YELLOW WOOD SORREL (*Oxalis corniculata*), is a very common plant found along road sides, in barn yards and cultivated ground. The flower has five deep yellow petals with yellow stamens. The leaf is divided into three leaflets, heart-shaped and acid to the taste. Flower is succeeded by small pods with points at ends. Blossoms May-September.

WHITE WOOD SORREL   YELLOW WOOD SORREL

FRINGED POLYGALA

MILKWORT FAMILY
(Polygalaceae)

This family is composed mostly of herbs with irregular flowers of three petals, the middle one of which often bears a crest. Its leaves are usually alternate.

FRINGED POLYGALA (*Polygala paucifolia*), is found in rich moist woods, in light soil. It grows low and its stem bears one or two flowers at the extreme tip. These flowers are large and winged, of a magenta color. They have three petals which are brought together to form a tube, and at the end of the tube, is a fringe. Its upper leaves are broad, large and crowded, near the flower; its lower leaves are small, scale-like and scattered. It is found from Maine south to Georgia, west to Illinois and Minnesota. Blossoms May-July.

JEWEL WEED FAMILY
(Balsaminaceae)

The members of this family are herbs with juicy stems, toothed leaves and irregular flowers which are interesting because one of the sepals is a sac.

THE SPOTTED TOUCH-ME-NOT (*Impatiens biflora*), is a common member of this family, so called because if one touches the seed-pod, when almost ripe, it "explodes" and scatters the seeds. The flower is orange color dotted with reddish brown spots. One of the sepals is an inflated sac, cone-shaped and ending in a spur about half the length of the sac. The leaves are delicate green, whitish underneath — taking on a silver sheen when held under water. Found in moist shaded places throughout United States. Blossoms July-September.

THE SPOTTED TOUCH-ME-NOT

ROUND-LEAVED MALLOW

MALLOW FAMILY
(Malvaceae)

ROUND-LEAVED MALLOW; CHEESES
(*Malva rotundifolia*), has flowers of
pinkish color, with five notched petals,
growing in clusters on long stems emerging from leaf-angles. Leaves are dark
green and round, five-lobed, toothed—
heart-shaped, on very long foot stalks. Its
seed receptacles resemble round "cheeses."
The Round-Leaved Mallow is a creeping
plant, considered a weed in gardens and
other cultivated ground. Common in
waste places etc. Blossoms June-October.

MALLOW ROSE; SWAMP ROSE MALLOW
(*Hibiscus Moscheutos*), has flowers of
rose-pink, four to seven inches across,
with five large petals, veined. Leaves
are tapered and olive-green, having three
lobes. Grows in brackish marshes, along
shores of deep waters. Blossoms August-
September.

VIOLET FAMILY
(Violaceae)

CANADA VIOLET *(Viola Canadensis)*, is a very common species throughout the United States. It has a faint fragrance and the heart-shaped, deep green leaves of the common violet. They are of a deep purple shade inside and lighter outside, side petals bearded. Blossoms May-July in moist woods everywhere.

COMMON VIOLET *(Viola papilionacea)*, is a robust little plant with deep violet petals, whitish at the base. The heart-shaped, deep-green leaves grow on long stems rising from the base of the plant. Found in moist meadows and woods, near civilization, extreme Northeast, southward and west to Minnesota; low grounds everywhere. Blossoms April-June.

CANADA VIOLET   COMMON VIOLET

41

VIOLET FAMILY (Cont.)
(Violaceae)

DOWNY VIOLET   BIRD-FOOT VIOLET

Downy Violet *(Viola pubescens)*, is a violet of the woods. It is tall; its stem and leaves are hairy. Flowers are small and yellow, veined with purple, side petals, bearded. Grows in damp woods from extreme Northeast, south to Texas and west to Nebraska. Blossoms April-May.

Bird-foot Violet *(Viola pedata)*, has cut leaves, divided into segments which are long and narrow. The upper petals of the beautiful flower are deep violet, the others paler, shading to lilac-purple and without beard. Anthers are orange-color and large, making the heart of the flower conspicuous. Found growing on sunny hillsides, in sandy soil of flat lands. Blossoms April-June.

EVENING PRIMROSE FAMILY
(Onagraceae)

Herbs with four petals and from four to eight stamens.

EVENING PRIMROSE *Oenothera biennis)*, is a tall, stout plant, erect, hairy and somewhat coarse. It has large, bright yellow flowers that unfold in the evening and fade in the morning. The four petals are rounded at the edges and the flowers are arranged along the stalk, the lower ones opening first, and lasting until mid-morning of the next day. Leaves are tapering, lance-shaped, sharp at the end, long, pale green and slightly toothed. Grows beside roads and in fields everywhere east of the Rockies. Blossoms July-August. An interesting fact about this primrose is that one may see the flower unfolding at about the same time every evening.

EVENING PRIMROSE

PARSLEY FAMILY
(Umbelliferae)

Some members of this family are very poisonous; others, innocent. Herbs, hollow stems, cut-leaves, clustered flowers.

WILD CARROT; QUEEN ANNE'S LACE; BIRD'S NEST *Daucus Carota).* The beauty of this wild plant depends, not upon its color, but upon the graceful arrangement of its flowers and its fine, cut leaves. The flowers are white and are arranged in flat clusters at the ends of the stems, each flower radiating from the center and making a pattern as lacey and fine as any Queen could desire. It is a first cousin to the garden carrot and resembles it. When the flower cluster grows old, it closes and looks like a bird's nest. Blossoms July-September in waste places everywhere.

WILD CARROT

44

HEATH FAMILY
(Ericaceae)

This is a family of shrubs and herbs with flowers usually regular, whose fruit is a capsule or a berry. It is a very large family. Among its best known members, are the cranberry and blueberry.

INDIAN PIPE *(Monotropa Uniflora)*, is a parasite whose bell-shaped flower has wedge-shaped, scale-like petals of delicate pink and nods in its solitary position. Sometimes, but rarely, two flowers are found on a stem. The plant is white and has "scales" instead of leaves. Lives in the dim seclusion of thick woods, on decaying vegetable matter. Found in the extreme Northeast, west to Arizona and Oregon and south. Blossoms July-August.

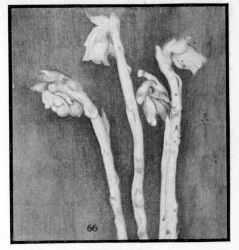

INDIAN PIPE

HEATH FAMILY (Cont.)
(Ericaceae)

WINTERBERRY **TRAILING ARBUTUS**

WINTERBERRY or TEABERRY *(Gaultheria procumbens)*. Found in evergreen forests and has a shiny, broad, evergreen leaf. Its flowers are wax-white and nod from leaf-angles. Berry is deep red and very aromatic. Blossoms July-August in woods from extreme Northeast, southward and westward.

TRAILING ARBUTUS *(Epigaea repens)*, a beautiful little plant, blossoming early in the spring, before the snow is melted. The flowers are very small, exquisite, rose-pink, and grow in clusters on a trailing, shrubby plant whose leaves are evergreen and heart-shaped. Flower has a very sweet, penetrating fragrance. Blossoms April-May—in extreme Northeast and south as far as the Gulf and west to Minnesota.

HEATH FAMILY (Cont.)
(Ericaceae)

WHITE SWAMP HONEYSUCKLE (*Rhododendron viscosum*), grows in swamps and has beautiful, showy flowers. Its leaves are rough-hairy, lance-shaped and blunt. Its flowers, appearing after or with the leaves, are either pure white or tinged with pink. They are very fragrant. This honeysuckle is found from the Northeast to Virginia, southwest to Arkansas. Blossoms June-July.

GREAT LAUREL (*Rhododendron maximum*), is a tall plant or shrub bearing beautiful flowers. (R. maximum was chosen as West Virginia's state flower and R. Californicum, the Washington state flower.) The great laurel has shiny, green leaves, evergreen, and its flowers, pale pink freckled with gold, cluster at the top of the stem. Blossoms June-July—in damp, deep woods, throughout the Alleghanies as far south as Georgia.

WHITE SWAMP HONEYSUCKLE

GREAT LAUREL

47

HEATH FAMILY (Cont.)
(Ericaceae)

SHIN LEAF (*Pyrola elliptica*). This is a very common species. The dull leaves are evergreen and the fragrant flowers nod on a long, upright stalk. They are white with five petals, an extremely long pistil and yellow anthers. Found in woods and thickets from the Northeast, south to New England States, west to Wisconsin. Blossoms June-July.

PINK AZALEA; PINXTER FLOWER (*Rhododendron nudiflorum*). Leaves of this species are somewhat hairy and of a yellowish-green color. Terminal flower clusters of flesh color, pink to purple at base of corolla-tube. Found in open woods and in moist, low places. Flowers precede leaves or come at the same time. Blossoms April-May. Found in Massachusetts, south to Texas, west to Illinois.

SHIN LEAF   **PINK AZALEA**

PRIMROSE FAMILY
(Primulaceae)

STAR FLOWER (*Trientalis Americana*), is a frail little plant that grows in the shade and is sometimes called "Star Anemone." Its leaves are light green, lance-shaped, tapering at both ends and growing in a whorl. It bears a delicate, white, star-shaped flower with a golden-yellow center. Blossoms May-June—and is found in the Northeast, west to Minnesota and southward and also in thin woods of White Mountains.

SHOOTING STAR (*Dodecatheon Meadia*), has a small cluster of rose-colored (sometimes white) flowers, pendulous from the tall flower-stalk. The five corolla divisions are turned backward, leaving exposed the golden-yellow anthers. The green leaves are clustered at the base of the plant. Found in woods, on hillsides and prairies. Blossoms April-May.

STAR FLOWER   SHOOTING STAR

PRIMROSE FAMILY (Cont.)
(Primulaceae)

PIMPERNEL (*Anagallis arvensis*), commonly called "Poor Man's Weather Glass," is a native of England and won its nickname because its scarlet or white flowers close quickly when bad weather approaches. It has five stamens and its filament* is bearded. It is a low, spreading herb with ovate, stemless leaves which grow opposite each other in pairs. Grows in sandy, waste places along Eastern coast. Blossoms June-August.

*A filament is the stalk of a stamen.

FRINGED LOOSESTRIFE (*Steironema ciliatum*), has a golden yellow flower divided into five parts, each one having a sharp twisted tip. Its leaves are smooth, pointed, lance-shaped and grow opposite to each other on the plant-stalk. Found in low places in the Northeast, west to Minnesota and Illinois, south to Virginia. Blossoms June-July.

PIMPERNEL   FRINGED LOOSESTRIFE

LOGANIA FAMILY
(Loganiaceae)

The Logania Family consists of herbs, shrubs or trees. Its leaves are opposite and its flowers are perfect.

INDIAN PINK; PINK ROOT (*Spigelia marilandica*), is an herb found in shady places — rich woods; flower is tubular, red outside, with five yellowish lobes. Grows up one side of stalk. Found from Ohio, south to Texas and Florida. Blossoms May-June.

YELLOW (FALSE) JESSAMINE (*Gelsemium sempervirens*), has a climbing stem, shining, ovate leaves, and as its Latin name implies, is evergreen—or almost so. Its flowers, large and fragrant, are yellow, arranged in clusters and shaped like funnels. They grow up one side of the spike. The Yellow Jessamine is found throughout the south, in low grounds, from Virginia to Florida and Texas.

INDIAN PINK   YELLOW FALSE
                       JESSAMINE

GENTIAN FAMILY
(Gentianaceae)

The Gentian Family is composed of herbs with bitter juices. It has regular flowers and simple leaves, which usually grow opposite to each other. The leaves are sessile*.

FRINGED GENTIAN *(Gentiana crinita)*, is one of the most beautiful and highly prized of all of our wild flowers. The flower is formed like a deep vase with a rounded, blue body. At the top of the vase-shaped flower, are four rounded lobes of voilet-blue, deeply fringed. When clouds obscure the sunshine and at night, the flowers close in a twisted shape. Leaves are yellowish-green. Grows in moist places from the Northeast to the Dakotas, south to the mountains in Georgia. Blossoms September-October.
*Sessile—without footstalk.

FRINGED GENTIAN

GENTIAN FAMILY (Cont.)
(Gentianaceae)

BOTTLE or CLOSED GENTIAN (*Gentiana Andrewsii*), so called because its blue flower is bottle-shaped and the corolla is tightly closed. Flowers are arranged in terminal clusters in axils of last pair of leaves. Leaves are smooth, lance-shaped, long, tapering at the end, arranged in pairs, opposite each other. Found in moist ground, in rich woods or along their edges. It blossoms August-October in the extreme Northeast, southward and westward.

LARGE MARSH PINK (*Sabatia dodecandra*), has a handsome, rose-pink or purplish flower, slender stems and wheel shaped corolla, with yellow center; each petal has a greenish yellow base, outlined with a crimson border. It is found in sandy places, on shores of brackish ponds. Blossoms July-August.

BOTTLE or CLOSED GENTIAN

MILKWEED FAMILY
(Asclepiadaceae)

COMMON MILKWEED

These plants have a milky juice which exudes when the stem is broken. The most common member is:

COMMON MILKWEED *(Asclepias syriaca)* The stem is tall, strong and soft-hairy. The light, yellowish-green leaves are broad and oblong, slightly hairy. The flowers grow in clusters emerging from the fork where the leaf-stem joins the plant-stem. Each blossom is tiny, shading from pale lavender to deep lilac. Later, the seed pod is filled with silky down with flat, yellowish seeds fastened to it. Common all over. Blossoms June-August. Ornamental. The milkweed is cultivated in England for garden purposes and is named among their garden flowers. It is decorative and forms an effective background.

MILKWEED FAMILY (Cont.)
(Asclepiadaceae)

Poke Milkweed (*Asclepias phytolac-coides*), is a taller species, with pendulous flower-clusters which are ivory white. Leaves are ovate and pointed at both ends, a trifle downy underneath. Found along hedges and moist places in extreme Northeast, south to Georgia, Arkansas and west to Minnesota. Blossoms June-August.

Butterfly Weed or Pleurisy Root (*Asclepias tuberosa*), bears brilliant orange flowers, arranged in flat, terminal clusters. It has very little of the milky juice common to other members of its family. Its leaves are short-stemmed, oblong and of a pale olive-green color, slightly hairy underneath Grows in dry pastures everywhere. Very common, especially through the south. Blossoms June-September.

POKE MILKWEED   BUTTERFLY WEED

CONVOLVULUS FAMILY
(Convolvulaceae)

The members of the Convolvulus Family climb and twine or trail, and have bell-shaped flowers, twisted in the bud. The leaves are alternate and the fruit is a globular capsule.

HEDGE BINDWEED; WILD MORNING GLORY *(Convolvulus sepium)*, is a leafy vine which twines about the nearest object. The flower is very beautiful, shaped like a funnel or bell, color varying from white to pale pink, the stamens showing yellow. Calyx has five parts. Flower opens in the morning and closes later in the day. The leaf is rather silver-green, shaped like an arrowhead, pointed at the end. Very ornamental. Grows along highways of the Northeast, south to North Carolina and west to Dakota and Utah. Blossoms June-August.

HEDGE BINDWEED

PHLOX FAMILY
(Polemoniaceae)

Most of the species of the Phlox Family are cultivated in our gardens. The Greek word equivalent to our "phlox," means "flame."

GROUND or MOSS PINK *(Phlox subulata)*, grows low and spreading, has thick, awl-shaped leaves and pinkish-purple flowers, growing in terminal clusters, few in each cluster. Grows in sandy soil and rocky hills, New York, west to Michigan, south to Florida. Blossoms April-September.

DOWNY PHLOX *(Phlox pilosa)*. The flowers of this species grow in a flat cluster at the top of the stem and are pinkish-purple. Leaves and stems are covered with downy hair. The lance-shaped leaves alternate up and down the stem. Found in dry places from Connecticut south and westward. Blossoms May-June.

GROUND PHLOX   DOWNY PHLOX

VIRGINIA COWSLIP   **FORGET-ME-NOT**

BORAGE FAMILY
(Boraginaceae)

The Borage Family consists mostly of rough-hairy herbs.

VIRGINIA COWSLIP *(Mertensia Virginica)*, has light blue flowers, trumpet-shaped, with arrow-shaped anthers. The green leaves are almost stemless, alternate, veined and very smooth. Found on river-banks of the Northeast, west to Nebraska and southwest. Blossoms March-May.

FORGET-ME-NOT *(Myosotis scorpioides)*, a perennial plant with rough-hairy leaves and a tiny, sky-blue flower with yellow center. Leaves are lance-shaped and of a greyish-green color. Found in damp places in extreme Northeast, south and west. Escape from gardens; native of Europe. Blossoms May-July.

VERVAIN FAMILY
(Verbenaceae)

The Vervain Family consists of herbs or shrubs whose leaves are opposite and whose flowers are irregular. When ripe, the fruit of the plant splits into nutlets, each nutlet having one seed. This family thrives in the tropics but is not so largely represented in the cooler places.

BLUE VERVAIN *(Verbena hastata)*, is the best known of this family. It is a tall plant; its flowers, tiny, purple and tube-shaped, grow on slender spikes, the whole effect of the flowering part of the plant being somewhat like a candelabrum. Its leaves are short-stemmed, lance-shaped, taper-pointed, rough and sharply toothed; the lower ones are usually divided into lobes. Found in damp places everywhere. Blossoms July-September.

BLUE VERVAIN

OSWEGO TEA

MINT FAMILY
(Labiatae)

This is a large family of aromatic herbs whose glands are supplied with oil.

OSWEGO TEA; BEE BALM (*Monarda didyma*), has a somewhat hairy stem, lance-shaped leaves, flower, slightly hairy. This plant strikes an arresting note when in blossom because of the brilliant red flowers it bears. The flower-heads, terminating the stems, are divided into florets, each one shaped like a tube, with long, pointed upper lip; the lower lip is divided into three parts, the one in the middle being longer than the ones on the sides. Usually these florets are scattered rather scantily over the head, but make a bright showing. Found in shady places in New England States, south and west. Blossoms July-September.

MINT FAMILY (Cont.)
(Labiatae)

CATNIP *(Nepeta Cataria)*, is a very common member of the Mint Family; its foliage, aromatic, is pleasing to the taste of cats. Hollow-stemmed plant has heart-shaped leaves, oblong, indented, whitish down underneath. Flower is whitish and grows in clusters. Thrives near civilization and blossoms July-September.

GROUND IVY; GILL-OVER-THE-GROUND *(Nepeta hederacea)*, is a small plant that creeps over the ground in country spaces. The leaves are round, kidney-shaped, their edges cut into round lobes and their surface soft-hairy and much veined. The flowers are tiny and purple, growing in small clusters. Blossoms May-July, throughout the eastern part of the United States, south to Georgia, west to Minnesota.

CATNIP   GROUND IVY

GREAT MULLEIN

FIGWORT FAMILY
(Scrophulariaceae)

Large family of bitter herbs, some narcotic, poisonous.

GREAT MULLEIN *(Verbascum Thapsus),* is a very common member of the Figwort Family. It grows to a height of six feet under favorable conditions, along roadsides, in fields and in cultivated ground. Its stem is tall and stout, flanked by its large, densely woolly leaves of a silver-green color. Flowers grow in a spike terminating the stem, and are yellow with golden-yellow centers. The leaves at the base of the plant are arranged in the form of a rosette. Corolla has five lobes and five stamens. This plant is cultivated in gardens in certain parts of England. Its leaves, dried and steeped, are supposed to have medicinal value. Blossoms June-September, in the extreme Northeast, south and west to Minnesota.

FIGWORT FAMILY (Cont.)
(Scrophulariaceae)

BLUE TOADFLAX (*Linaria Canadensis*), is a slender, smooth plant with tiny, tube-shaped flowers of blue-violet, with spur and two lips, upper one with two lobes, under one with three. Common in dry, flat places throughout the United States. Blossoms June-September.

MONKEY FLOWER (*Mimulus ringens*), has lance-shaped leaves arranged opposite each other and of a light green color. The flower is purple, its corolla having two lips, the upper one two-lobed and the under one, three-lobed. At the mouth of the flower are two bright yellow spots. Found in damp places extreme Northeast, south to Virginia and Tennessee, west to South Dakota, Minnesota, Nebraska, Texas and in California. Blossoms June-September.

BLUE TOADFLAX   MONKEY FLOWER

63

FIGWORT FAMILY (Cont.)
(Scrophulariaceae)

TOADFLAX

TOADFLAX; BUTTER AND EGG PLANT (*Linaria vulgaris*), is one of the best known of this family. Its yellow flower is tube-shaped, having upper and under lip, the upper with two lobes, the under with three lobes, the middle one of which is pouch-shaped and ends in a spur. Center is yellow. Throat of the flower is almost closed by orange-colored projection. Its leaves are light green and smooth. Blossoms in waste places everywhere July-October.

SMALL SNAPDRAGON (*Antirrhinum Orontium*), a slender annual with smooth, long and narrow leaves. Its flower, purple and white, grows solitary upon its stem and has a two-lipped corolla, the upper one, two-lobed, the under one, three-lobed. Found in waste places in the extreme Northeast. Blossoms June-August.

FIGWORT FAMILY (Cont.)
(Scrophulariaceae)

SCARLET PAINTED CUP; INDIAN PAINT BRUSH *(Castilleja coccinea),* is a hairy plant, its root-leaves clustered; those of the stem are cut sharply. They are light green, usually soft-hairy. The calyx of the flower is long and cylindrical, extending upward about the corolla, almost hiding it. It has two lobes and at its tip, it is stained a brilliant scarlet. The corolla is so insignificant as to be almost unworthy of mention. It is of a pale yellowish color. Contrary to usual facts, it is not the blossom of this plant which makes it conspicuous and beautiful, but its scarlet floral leaves. Common in waste places—meadows, damp grounds of the extreme Northeast, south to Virginia and Kentucky and throughout western United States. Blossoms June-July. It has a parasitic root.

SCARLET PAINTED CUP

TURTLEHEAD   PURPLE GERARDIA

FIGWORT FAMILY (Cont.)
(Scrophulariaceae)

TURTLEHEAD *(Chelone glabra)*, has lance-shaped, sharp-toothed leaves and large, white or purple, clustered flowers. The upper lip of the tube-shaped corolla is ridged, woolly in the throat, the under lip having three lobes. Blossoms July-September in moist places of the extreme Northeast, southward, west to Minnesota, Kansas, Texas.

PURPLE GERARDIA *(Gerardia purpurea)*, has flowers of bright purple, is very hairy and has spreading branches. Its leaves are long and narrow with rough edges. They are small, of a yellow-green color and quite pointed at the tips. Flower is funnel-shaped, its mouth spreading into five lobes which are freckled and hairy inside. Anthers are orange-color. Blossoms August-October from Massachusetts, south to Florida and Texas, west to Wisconsin.

FIGWORT FAMILY (Cont.)
(Scrophulariaceae)

FALSE PIMPERNEL *(Ilysanthes dubia)*. The corolla of this species has an upper and lower lip, the upper having two lobes and the lower, three lobes. The plant, branching and spreading, has ovate leaves with toothed edges. The pale purple flowers grow on long and slender stalks. Thrives in low, moist ground everywhere. Blossoms July-September.

PENTSTEMON or BEARD-TONGUE *(Pentstemon hirsutus)*, has pale green leaves, slightly woolly, lance-shaped and toothedged. The flowers are pinkish-white, the corolla is trumpet-shaped, having two lips, upper with two lobes and lower with three lobes. Found in dry and rocky places — open woods and hedges — from extreme Northeast, southward and west to Wisconsin. Blossoms May-July.

FALSE PIMPERNEL   PENTSTEMON

ENGLISH PLANTAIN   COMMON PLANTAIN

PLANTAIN FAMILY
(Plantaginaceae)

This is not an interesting family, but some of its members are so common that we should be able to name them.

ENGLISH PLANTAIN; RIB GRASS *(Plantago lanceolata)*, though somewhat similar to the following, has lance-shaped, narrower leaves radiating from the base, the stems deeply grooved. The flower-spike is short and bears tiny, dull white flowers. Found everywhere in waste places. Blossoms April-October.

COMMON PLANTAIN *(Plantago major)*, is so general and hardy that it is a weed. Its leaves are large, somewhat heart-shaped and ribbed, thick and tough. The flower stalk is tall and cylindrical, with tiny white flowers on it. Found in waste places everywhere. Blossoms June-September.

MADDER FAMILY
(Rubiaceae)

LARGE HOUSTONIA (*Houstonia purpurea*), is slightly hairy and its leaves vary from heart-shaped to lance-shaped. Taller than the following; tubular, lavender flowers cluster in small groups. In thin woods from Maryland, south to Alabama and westward to Arkansas. Blossoms May-July.

BLUETS; HOUSTONIA (*Houstonia caerulea*), sometimes called "Innocence." The corolla of the flower is funnel-shaped and has four lobes, spreading at its top. Corolla is white or the lobes are light blue or violet and the center is golden-yellow. Leaves are slightly heart-shaped, growing in pairs on very slender, thread-like stems, larger and massed at roots. Found in waste places in extreme North-east, south to Georgia and Alabama. west to Michigan. Blossoms April-July.

LARGE HOUSTONIA   **BLUETS**

69

MADDER FAMILY (Cont.)
(Rubiaceae)

PARTRIDGEBERRY

PARTRIDGEBERRY; TWINBERRY (*Mitchella repens*). Creeping about the feet of trees, we find the partridgeberry. It is a beautiful little evergreen vine, its flowers bell-shaped, white and fragrant, sometimes tinged with purple; in the fall these little flowers are followed by scarlet berries which last all winter. Its leaves are dark green, slightly heart-shaped and shining. Common in woods, especially among cone-bearing trees, from extreme Northeast, southward, westward to Wisconsin, Minnesota, Arkansas and Texas. Blossoms June-July.

SMALL BEDSTRAW (*Galium trifidum*), is a very small plant that branches freely and bears white flowers which have three lobes. Flowers are solitary or arranged in tiny clusters. Found everywhere in bogs and wet woods. Blossoms July-September.

HONEYSUCKLE FAMILY
(Caprifoliaceae)

The Honeysuckle Family is composed of shrubs, vines and, rarely, herbs, with opposite leaves. The fruit is a berry or a pod. The flowers are usually shaped like a funnel and are sought by insects and humming birds.

TWIN-FLOWER *(Linnaea borealis)*, is a slender, creeping, little evergreen vine, slightly hairy, with rounded leaves. The flower-stems rise along the vine, thread-like and erect, forking into two stems at the top, each bearing a beautiful, fragrant, solitary flower, bell-shaped and nodding. Corolla flares into five lobes, and is whitish, tinted and striped with rose-pink or rose-purple. Found in mountains, moist, moss-grown woods from extreme Northeast, westward to Washington, South Dakota and Colorado. Blossoms June-August.

TWIN-FLOWER

HONEYSUCKLE FAMILY (Cont.)
(Caprifoliaceae)

TRUMPET

Trumpet or Coral Honeysuckle (*Lonicera sempervirens*), is a climbing vine. Leaves are nearly smooth, oblong and deep green. Flowers grow in whorls and are tubular, terminating the spike. They are a reddish color outside, yellowish inside, with five lobes at top. The top leaves are united into one round leaf, through which the stem, seemingly, penetrates. In the south, the leaves of the Trumpet Honeysuckle remain green throughout the year. This species is widely cultivated in gardens, not only for its blossoms but for its ornamental berries. Is very attractive to humming birds. Grows in copses from Northeast, westward to Nebraska and southward. Flowers are followed by vivid red berry. Blossoms April-August.

GOURD FAMILY
(Cucurbitaceae)

The Gourd Family is composed chiefly of herbs with tendrils and with alternate leaves. It bears fleshy or membranous fruit.

CLIMBING WILD CUCUMBER; WILD BALSAM APPLE (*Echinocystis lobata*), is a climbing, luxuriant vine, very decorative and fragrant. It has thin leaves, divided into lobes which come to a point. Flowers have six petals, are greenish-white and united at the base into a spreading corolla. They grow in clusters. The vine has three forked tendrils which twine about objects. It bears a fruit which is egg-shaped, green, with weak prickles scattered over its outside surface. Found on river banks, in cultivated grounds and in waste places of the extreme Northeast, west to South Dakota, and Texas. Blossoms July-September. Greek name means "Hedge-hog" and "bladder."

CLIMBING WILD CUCUMBER

73

80

BELLFLOWER

BELLFLOWER FAMILY
(Campanulaceae)
(Bluebell Family)

The Bellflower Family consists of herbs with alternate leaves; the flowers are solitary and terminal or grow in a spike. They are usually bell-shaped and from this fact, the family derives its name, as the Italian word for bell is "campana."

BELLFLOWER *(Campanula rapunculoides)*, has a very slender stem, smooth, slightly hairy above; lower leaves are round-oblong and heart-shaped; upper, round-oblong and lance-shaped. The cup-shaped, nodding, purple flowers have five lobes, usually the majority of them growing on one side of the stem. Calyx is rough-hairy, turning backwards. Grows in fields and beside roads. Sometimes finds its way into gardens. Found in the extreme Northeast. Blossoms June-September.

74

BELLFLOWER FAMILY (Cont.)

(Campanulaceae)
(Bluebell Family)

HAREBELL or BLUEBELL (*Campanula rotundifolia*), is a slender plant, perennial, with round, heart-shaped leaves clustering at its base, tooth-edged and dropping early. The stem-leaves are long and narrow, nearly lance-shaped. Has a tall, wiry flower-stem, upon which grow violet-blue, bell-shaped flowers, nodding from thread-like stems and spreading in five lobes; center, pale lavender. The Harebell, although a very dainty and delicate appearing plant, is so rugged that it can survive extreme cold. It varies greatly in height, the number of its flowers and the profuseness of its branching, in different environments. Found in mountains of the Northeast, South Dakota, Nebraska and the Rocky Mountains, California and Arizona. Blossoms June-September.

HAREBELL

LOBELIA FAMILY
(Lobeliaceae)

GREAT LOBELIA (*Lobelia syphilitica*). This species is somewhat hairy, having leaves of a pale green color, pointed at either end. The flowers are of a pale blue color. It grows in low grounds. Found in Maine, southward and westward. Blossoms July to late September.

CARDINAL FLOWER (*Lobelia cardinalis*), is one of the most striking and beautiful of our wild flowers. Its leaves are oblong and lance-shaped with toothed edges. The flower-spike is brilliant with remarkable red flowers, tubular, with two-lobed upper lip and three-lobed under lip, spreading and of a bright red color. It is found everywhere in low, wet places and strikes a brilliant note of color among the marsh grasses. Blossoms August-September.

GREAT LOBELIA   CARDINAL FLOWER

LOBELIA FAMILY (Cont.)
(Lobeliaceae)

KALM'S LOBELIA (*Lobelia Kalmii*), is small, grows low and has slender, branching stems. Flowers are light blue, arranged at the ends of the stems and branches on very slender stalks. Found from Newfoundland to New Jersey, west to Iowa, Minnesota, also in Ohio and Michigan. Blossoms July-September.

INDIAN TOBACCO (*Lobelia inflata*). Stem, hairy and branching. Leaves are oval and pointed, pale green and slightly toothed. Lower leaves are large, while those near the top are very small. It bears a violet-blue flower (sometimes lavender and white), very small, and poison fruit. Found in extreme Northeast, south and west. Grows in open fields, woods, moist grounds or dry soil. Blossoms July-October.

KALM'S LOBELIA   INDIAN TOBACCO

COMPOSITE FAMILY
(Compositae)

This is a very large family consistin of many beautiful and interesting flower The corolla is strap-shaped or tubula The flowers with a strap-shaped coroll are called ray-flowers, and the hea which bears these flowers is radiate. Th tubular flowers make up the disc. Th members of this family are mostly herb notable for their flower heads.

JOE-PYE-WEED; TRUMPET WEED *(Eup torium purpureum)*, has a tall, stout ste with oblong and ovate leaves, tooth-edge and of a pale green color, growing i whorls. It has a close head of sma pinkish florets, varying in depth of colo even to a whitish-pink. Flower cluste terminate the stems. Found everywhe in low, damp grounds, sometimes woods and thickets. Blossoms Augus September.

JOE-PYE-WEED

COMPOSITE FAMILY (Cont.)
(Compositae)

TALL BLAZING STAR (*Liatris scariosa*), has a long spike, ornamented with flower-heads of tubular flowers, shading from purple to lavender; leaves are dark green, lance-shaped and tapering toward the end. Very showy and beautiful. Found in dry soil of the Northeast, west to Nebraska and southwest to Texas. Blossoms August-September.

BONESET or THOROUGHWORT (*Eupatorium perfoliatum*), is a very common member of the Composite Family. It has a stout, hairy stem, with lance-shaped leaves, in pairs, united at the base so that two appear as one leaf with the stem perforating it. They are downy underneath and taper to a point. Florets grow in dull white, terminal clusters. "Boneset Tea" was a popular household remedy. Grows everywhere in moist places. Blossoms July-September.

TALL BLAZING STAR   BONESET

COMPOSITE FAMILY (Cont.)
(Compositae)

SEASIDE GOLDEN-ROD WHITE GOLDEN-ROD or
SILVER-ROD

SEASIDE GOLDEN-ROD *(Solidago semper-virens)*, is a smooth, stout plant with lance-shaped leaves. The flowers grow in short clusters and are golden-yellow. Effect is plume-like. Found in the extreme Northeast to Florida and westward. Grows in swamps and brackish wet places. Blossoms August-November.

WHITE GOLDEN-ROD or SILVER-ROD *(Solidago bicolor)*, is a very common species, distinguished because it is the only golden-rod that has white flowers. It is greyish-white with soft hairs. Its leaves are elliptical, lance-shaped, terminating with a sharp angle at both ends. The flowers are white or cream and grow in small clusters where the leaf-stem joins the plant-stem. Found in barren waste places, dry soil, in extreme Northeast, south to Georgia and west to Missouri. Blossoms August-September.

COMPOSITE FAMILY (Cont.)
(Compositae)

ROUGH-STEMMED GOLDEN-ROD (*Solidago rugos1*), has a hairy stem and leaves, crowded, lance-shaped, tapering toward the base, sharply toothed, dark green in color. The light yellow flower-heads are arranged in clusters and terminate the branching stem of the plant. Found everywhere in damp thickets and along roadsides. Blossoms July-September.

CANADA GOLDEN-ROD (*Solidago Canadensis*), has a slender stem with narrow, lance-shaped leaves, smooth on top and slightly hairy underneath. Flowers are greenish-yellow, arranged in dense, small heads which crowd together on the downward curving plumes. This is a coarse, tall species, not noticeable for its beauty. Grows in rich ground, copses, highways, everywhere. Blossoms August-October.

ROUGH-STEMMED GOLDEN-ROD

COMPOSITE FAMILY (Cont.)
(Compositae)

EARLY GOLDEN-ROD

EARLY GOLDEN-ROD *(Solidago juncea)*, is a slender, smooth plant with long, lower lance-shaped leaves, sharply toothed; upper leaves are lance-shaped, narrow and tapering, all of yellow-greenish color. Flower clusters, dense with golden yellow flowers, curve downward. Found in dry ground, thickets, banks, in the extreme Northeast, south to North Carolina and west to Missouri. Blossoms from June-September.

BLUE-STEMMED GOLDEN-ROD *(Solidago caesia)*, is a very graceful species that carries its bloom in oblong clusters at the fork where the leaf joins the stem. It has lance-shaped leaves, sharply toothed and pointed, of a dark green color. It is common everywhere and may be found along the edges of woods or other shady places. Blossoms August-October.

COMPOSITE FAMILY (Cont.)
(Compositae)

LANCE-LEAVED GOLDEN-ROD *(Solidago graminifolia)*, is unique among golden-rods. Its flower-clusters are not plume-like, but flat-topped (corymb-like) crowded with tiny, yellow flowers. Its stem is smooth and its leaves are lance-shaped, long and narrow. It has a faint and pleasant odor which does not character-ize other members of the family. Grows in damp ground everywhere and blossoms August-October.

SHOWY GOLDEN-ROD *(Solidago speci-osa)*, has a stout stem with thick, oval leaves, rough on the edges and of an olive-green color. Flower-heads are crowded in upstanding clusters, the whole forming a pyramid of golden-yellow color. Grows in thickets and rich grounds, open woods, extreme Northeast, southward and westward. Blossoms August-October.

LANCE-LEAVED GOLDEN-ROD

COMPOSITE FAMILY (Cont.)
(Compositae)

GOLDEN ASTER (*Chrysopsis graminifolia*), has a slender stem, bears few heads and has lance-shaped leaves, long and narrow, grass-like and hairy, also glossy. The flowers, which are very small and of a deep yellow in color, are composed of disc and ray-flowers. They are solitary and grow at the ends of the branches. This species is found in dry places from New Jersey and Delaware, southwest to Texas. Blossoms August-October.

GOLDEN ASTER (*Chrysopsis Mariana*), has a stout stem, hairy when young, smooth when old. Leaves are greyish-green and oblong. Flowers are golden-yellow. Grows in dry, sandy waste places from New York and Pennsylvania. Blossoms August-October.

GOLDEN ASTER   GOLDEN ASTER

COMPOSITE FAMILY (Cont.)
(Compositae)

NEW ENGLAND ASTER *(Aster Novae Angliae)*, has a stout, hairy stem with many lance-shaped, minutely-hairy, clasping leaves, toothless and yellow-green, heart-shaped near base. Purple flowers grow in large, terminal clusters and are very showy and beautiful. Grows in soil rich in lime-stone, Northeast, westward and southward. Blossoms August-October.

ASTER PATENS, is a very common species, rough and hairy, with its branches spreading widely. Most of its heads are solitary, borne at the ends of the branches, and having deep purple rays. Its leaves are either oblong and lance-shaped or oval, rough on the edges; growing tight to the stalk, without stems. Found in dry places from Central Maine to Minnesota and southwest. Blossoms August-October.

NEW ENGLAND ASTER

87.

ASTER LINARIIFOLIUS

COMPOSITE FAMILY (Cont.)
(Compositae)

Aster Linariifolius, has stems rising from a woody root. The solitary flower terminate the branches and are of a pale violet color—rarely white. Its leaves are narrow, with rough margins and very numerous. This aster grows in dry places everywhere. Blossoms September-October.

Smooth Aster *(Aster laevis)*, is stout plant, bearing its flower-heads in closely arranged, terminal clusters, light blue or blue-violet in color, having from fifteen to twice that many rays. Leaves are thick, lance-shaped, with heart-shaped base. The upper ones are more or less clasping. This species varies in different localities, but is always very showy. Found in dry places and thin shade everywhere. Blossoms September-October.

COMPOSITE FAMILY (Cont.)
(Compositae)

HEART-LEAVED ASTER *(Aster cordifolius)*, has a nearly smooth stem, branching above and bearing many flower-heads. Its leaves are thin, sharply toothed, light green, rough to the touch, the lower ones being heart-shaped. The small flowers are numerous and densely crowded, with yellow centers surrounded by lilac colored rays. Common all over in woods and along shady borders. Blossoms September-October.

PANICLED ASTER *(Aster paniculatus)*, has a smooth, tall, branching stem with scattered heads of loosely arranged flowers with white or purple rays. The leaves are narrow, lance-shaped, lower ones slightly toothed, pointed. Grows in damp, low grounds and thinly shaded places everywhere. Blossoms August-October.

HEART-LEAVED ASTER

SHOWY ASTER

SHARP-LEAVED WOOD ASTER

COMPOSITE FAMILY (Cont.)
(Compositae)

SHOWY ASTER *(Aster spectabilis)*, is a very beautiful species with bright violet flowers and oblong, dark green, lance-shaped leaves, slightly rough. Flowers are large, having about twenty rays each. Grows in sandy soil, Massachusetts to Delaware along coast. Blossoms August-October.

SHARP-LEAVED WOOD ASTER *(Aster acuminatus)*, is a low-growing species, somewhat hairy, whose habitat is the woods. It has large flowers whose narrow rays are far apart and of a whitish-lilac color. Its leaves are oblong, lance-shaped, dark green, sharply toothed, short stemmed, pointed at both ends. They are alternate along the lower part of the stem, but arranged below the flower, almost in a complete circle. Found in the East, south to Georgia. Blossoms August-September.

COMPOSITE FAMILY (Cont.)
(Compositae)

PURPLE CONE FLOWER *(Brauneria purburea)*, has a smooth or slightly hairy stem with rough, toothed leaves, the lowest ones ovate, the upper ones, ovate-lance-shaped. The flowers are very showy, supporting a flower head with a purple disk and numerous purple rays. Grows in rich soil, from Pennsylvania and Virginia to Michigan, Iowa, southward. Blossoms July-September.

ROBIN'S PLANTAIN *(Erigeron pulchellus)*, a very showy plant, has light green, hairy stem, bearing a few large heads on its slender flower stalks. Its leaves are somewhat toothed; some of them cluster in a dense tuft about the base of the plant. The rays are very numerous and of a light blue-purple color, with greenish-yellow center disk. Found on moist banks and thickets everywhere. Blossoms April-June.

PURPLE CONE FLOWER ROBIN'S PLANTAIN

OXEYE DAISY   **BLACK-EYED SUSAN**

COMPOSITE FAMILY (Cont.)
(Compositae)

OXEYE DAISY *(Chrysanthemum Leucanthemum)*, has an erect stem, the toothed leaves at the base gradually narrowing down from a broad summit, middle and upper leaves, oblong and coarsely toothed. Flower has golden-yellow center with pure white rays. Found in meadows and fields. Common. Blossoms June-September.

BLACK-EYED SUSAN; CONE FLOWER *(Rudbeckia hirta)*, is a very rough and hairy specimen, its stems stout and branching near its base. The brown disk of the single, large flower head is surrounded by very small florets, tubular in shape, which, when the pollen is ripe, make a yellow circle. Its golden-yellow rays curve slightly backward. Found in Northeast, west to South Dakota and southward. Blossoms June-September.

COMPOSITE FAMILY (Cont.)
(Compositae)

TEN-PETALED SUN FLOWER (*Helianthus decapetalus*), has a branching stem, smooth below and rough above; its leaves, rough or smooth, ovate, dark green and pointed, growing opposite, in pairs. Its flowers have ten or more yellow rays, a yellow disk, and are supported on thread-like stems. Found in the extreme Northeast in thickets, on banks of streams, southwest and west to Minnesota and Missouri. Blossoms August-September.

FEVERFEW (*Chrysanthemum Parthenium*), is a tall, branching, leafy species with small flowers, growing in clusters, with yellow disks composed of tiny florets; rays are white. Its leaves are cut—the divisions, ovate. Very ornamental. Found in gardens. Thrives in Massachusetts to New Jersey, west to Wisconsin. Blossoms June-September.

TEN-PETALED   FEVERFEW
SUNFLOWER

COMPOSITE FAMILY (Cont.)
(Compositae)

LARGER BUR-MARIGOLD　　**TANSY**

LARGER BUR-MARIGOLD; BROOK SUN-FLOWER *(bidens laevis)*, has a smooth stem, with lance-shaped leaves, tapering at both ends, toothed and without footstalk. Flowers have showy, golden-yellow rays. Common in wet places and along banks of running water in New England States and southwest. Blossoms August-October.

TANSY *(Tanacetum vulgare)*, has a smooth stem with cut leaves and small flowers with disks of tube-shaped, orange colored florets growing in flat-topped clusters; no rays. It has a strong, aromatic odor and a bitter taste. Usually thought to be an escape from old and deserted gardens. It is sometimes used in medicine as a bitter tonic. Found in the extreme Northeast, south to North Carolina and west to Dakota. Blossoms July-September.

COMPOSITE FAMILY (Cont.)
(Compositae)

BULL THISTLE (*Cirsium lanceolatum*). Very common. Has dark green leaves forming prickly margined wings, rough above and cottony below. The receptacle of the flower is equipped with soft bristles. Florets are tubular in shape, crowded in dense clusters, of a purple color, forming terminal heads. Fragrant. Found everywhere beside highways and in pastures. Blossoms July-October.

PASTURE THISTLE (*Cirsium pumilum*), has a very large, purple, fragrant flower. The stem is low and stout. The leaves are light green, oblong, lance-shaped, slightly hairy and divided into prickly-edged lobes. Grows in dry fields Northeast to Pennsylvania and Delaware. Blossoms July-September.

BULL THISTLE   PASTURE THISTLE

COMPOSITE FAMILY (Cont.)
(Compositae)

COMMON DANDELION

COMMON DANDELION (*Taraxacum offiinale*), is very common in pastures an fields, invades lawns and gardens, becom ing a pest. It has long, deeply-toothe leaves and bright yellow flowers, de gold in the center and paler gold alo the margin. One flower on a hollo stem. Flower later becomes a fluf globe of silky down. The leaves of t dandelion make very excellent gree and have tonic properties. They shou be gathered in early spring. Blossor May-June.

DWARF DANDELION (*Krigia Virginic* is a small plant, branching from the ba having toothed leaves; flower heads te minate the flower-stalks and are of bright yellow color. Grows in dry plac Northeast, west to Minnesota. Blosso April-August.

INDEX

95